20 Minute
Desserts
& After Dinner Treats

Acknowledgements

Alison's Choice for high quality dried fruit, nuts and seeds.

Benniks Poultry Farm, Buller Road, Levin, for RSPCA approved barn-laid eggs.

Kapiti Cheeses Ltd for their prize-winning cheeses.

William Aitken Ltd for **Lupi** olive oils, infused olive oils, grapeseed oil and balsamic vinegar.

Zespri for Green and Gold kiwifruit.

Thanks to the following Wellington stores, **Freedom** and **Living & Giving**, who provided the beautiful tableware used in the photographs. Specifically this was from:

Freedom: glass page 5; glasses page 15; napkin page 16; glasses, table mat, napkin & plate page 21; candles & glass page 27; cutlery, glasses & placemat page 37; plate page 38; trivet page 41; plate & glasses page 47; flowers page 49; placemat & napkin page 53; cup & saucer page 55.

Living & Giving: plate & spoon page 5; spoons page 15; glass bowls & spoons page 16; spoon page 19; glass plate page 31; coffee spoons page 41; blue glass plate page 49; glass bowls & plate page 53; plate page 55.

About This Book

We would be the first to admit that neither desserts nor after dinner treats are an essential part of our everyday lives!

We do feel, however, that there are many times when a dessert or little treat after the main course of the evening meal is called for. Perhaps it is a birthday or special anniversary, or somebody at your dining table has good reason to celebrate some major (or minor) triumph. Sometimes a sumptuous dessert can make good friends feel especially welcome. On the other hand, after a day when nothing good has happened, an unexpected treat can make everyone feel better!

On a more mundane level, it is sometimes good to have a dessert to fill up empty corners after a less substantial main course, or to add more fruit or dairy products to your family's daily quota.

We found it a bit tricky to know exactly what we should include in our 20 minute time frame. While many desserts can be made from start to finish and be ready to eat in 20 minutes, a few are very quick to prepare but need to be left to look after themselves in the refrigerator or oven before being brought to the table.

It is always hard to know exactly how long it takes someone else to prepare food. We know these recipes well, and know they can be made in 20 minutes or less (barring distractions by the phone, kids, etc.). When you try a recipe for the first time, however, it may take you considerably longer than it will after you have made it a couple of times – persevere and you'll be surprised just how fast many of these can be made.

This said, here are a few tips to help you speed up preparation:

- Read your recipe and check what you already have, before you go shopping. Take the recipe (or recipes!) you plan to cook when you go shopping – just pop this little book in your bag!

- Read the recipe from beginning to end, before you start.

- Get out all the ingredients you need and arrange them in the order in which you will use them.

We hope you'll find these recipes useful and enjoy them as much as we do!

Happy cooking,
Simon Holst & Alison Holst

Instant Strawberry Ice Cream

This ice cream is ready to eat one minute after you start making it. Either freeze the fruit or berry of your choice in packets containing 2 cups, or buy frozen berries. You must use free-flow, hard frozen berries cut in thumb-nail size cubes when making the ice cream.

FOR 3-4 SERVINGS:
2 cups frozen (diced) free-flow
  strawberries
½ cup icing sugar
about ½ cup chilled cream, milk or
  yoghurt

Chop berries into 5mm–1cm cubes. Fruit MUST be frozen hard, free-flow and in small pieces when used. Tip into food processor bowl. Work quickly to keep fruit very cold. Process with metal chopping blade until fruit is finely chopped (10–20 seconds). This is a noisy operation. Without delay, add the icing sugar and process briefly until mixed.

With machine running, add the chilled liquid of your choice through the feed-tube in a fine stream, until a smooth, frozen cream has formed. The amount needed varies from batch to batch. Stop as soon as the mixture is evenly textured and creamy.

Serve ice cream made with chilled milk or yoghurt immediately. Ice cream made with cream may be frozen for later use if desired.

VARIATION: Replace icing sugar with low calorie sweetener if desired. Experiment with other berries, berry mixtures and cubed raw fruit.

NOTE: Berries with many seeds are not successful and bland fruits do not make memorable ice cream.

Sugar-dusted Crisps

These are fun, deliciously crunchy, and a little different! They are especially good served with ice cream or other soft textured foods.

Use fresh or thawed wonton skins. Leave them whole, or cut them diagonally or in strips. Heat about a cup of grapeseed or canola oil, preferably in a wok (or in a smallish pot), until it is hot enough to fry a piece of wonton in 40–50 seconds.

Drop in wontons one, two or three at a time, depending on size of pieces and the container. Turn if necessary to lightly brown all sides. When frying whole wontons, pinch them into interesting folds with tongs while they cook.

When evenly golden brown, drain on paper towels, dust with sieved icing sugar and serve as soon as possible (or store in airtight plastic bags).

Passionfruit Panacotta with Grilled Nectarines

This quickly made dessert must be prepared several hours before you need it – overnight is good. We like it with ripe nectarines grilled at the last minute, or with fresh berries.

FOR FOUR ½ CUP SERVINGS:
¼ cup orange juice
3 level tsp gelatine
¼ cup sugar
¼ cup passionfruit pulp
1¼ cups cream
½ cup milk
1 tsp vanilla essence

Stir orange juice and gelatine together in a small container and leave to soften. Meanwhile, stir the sugar and passionfruit pulp together in a pot over low heat until the sugar dissolves. Take off heat and stir in the softened gelatine until it melts. Stir the cream into the warm mixture. Add the milk and vanilla. Stand the pot in a bigger bowl containing cold water and ice blocks and cool, stirring frequently until mixture thickens enough to hold up the passionfruit seeds. Pour into four clean, wetted glasses, plastic glasses or bowls, each of which holds about ½ a cup. Refrigerate for at least 4 hours.

When panacottas have set well, warm the sides and base of each container briefly by dipping in warm water. Tilt container and run a thin knife blade between each pudding and its container to help the pudding slip out, then turn out onto flat plates. Pour a little bought passionfruit yoghurt topping or flavouring, or homemade coulis (see following recipe) over each dessert just before serving with the grilled nectarines, and the rest of the coulis in a bowl.

Passionfruit Coulis

Chop two peeled nectarines or peaches into thin slices. Simmer in ¼ cup of orange juice for 5–10 minutes, then purée fruit and liquid until smooth. Stir in 2–4 tablespoons of passionfruit pulp (or topping), leave to cool, then thin to pouring consistency with extra juice if necessary.

Grilled Nectarines

Preheat grill five minutes before starting to cook. Halve ripe nectarines (one per person) and remove stones. Dip cut surface in a little orange or lemon juice. Place cut side up on a shallow pan lined with lightly buttered foil. Sprinkle fruit with sugar, allowing about a teaspoon per half. Grill 10–12cm from heat until cut surface is golden brown, probably about 5 minutes.

Kiwifruit Tiramisu

Contrasting layers of diced kiwifruit, coffee-soaked cake and marscapone-cream served in tall glasses ensure this easy dessert looks as good as it tastes.

FOR ABOUT 8 SERVINGS:

8–12 Zespri Green kiwifruit
caster sugar, optional
300g (about 1¼ cups) marscapone
1 Tbsp brandy, coffee or orange liqueur
¼ cup caster sugar
1 cup cream, lightly whipped
4 tsp instant coffee
1 cup sugar
½ cup hot water
400–500g Madeira cake, cubed
shaved or grated chocolate to garnish

Peel the Zespri Green kiwifruit, then quarter them lengthways and cut into 7–10mm thick slices. Sprinkle with a little caster sugar to sweeten slightly if desired.

Put the marscapone in a large bowl and stir in the brandy or liqueur and caster sugar (this should soften it nicely), then fold in the lightly whipped cream. Cover and set aside until required.

Stir the instant coffee, sugar and water together in a small pot (or microwave bowl). Bring to the boil and simmer for 2–3 minutes until the sugar dissolves. While the syrup cools, cut the Madeira cake into 1–2cm cubes. Place cubes in a shallow dish or tray and drizzle with the syrup, turning them gently so most sides are covered with syrup.

Arrange the sponge, kiwifruit and cream in alternate layers in individual glasses or other containers. Vary the order as you please. If you put sponge at the bottom it soaks up any excess liquid nicely. If you finish with a layer or dollop of the cream mixture, it looks great garnished with a little shaved or grated dark chocolate. (If desired, you can assemble these, except for the final layer, up to 8 hours in advance, then just cover and refrigerate until required.)

Raspberry Meringue Cream

Raspberries give tartness, flavour and a very pretty colour to this easily assembled, summery dessert. (Exact proportions are not essential.)

FOR 4-6 SERVINGS:
about 125g "bought" meringues
about 250g frozen or fresh raspberries
300ml cream, lightly whipped
½ tsp vanilla essence

Cut or break meringues into chunky 1cm cubes. Do not crumble finely.

Thaw frozen raspberries, putting a few perfect whole berries aside for a garnish. Break and mash the rest into smaller pieces as they become softer. (Larger amounts of berries make a pudding with a stronger fruit flavour.) The pudding is best assembled when the berries are almost completely thawed. If using fresh berries, slightly mash them with the back of a spoon. Do not purée the fresh or frozen berries.

In a large bowl, beat the cream with the vanilla until the mixture is just thick enough so that you cannot pour it from the bowl. Take care not to overbeat the cream until it looks dry. Using a spatula or stirrer, fold all the meringue pieces through the whipped cream, then fold the raspberries (and any raspberry juice) fairly evenly through the mixture. Leave a few streaks, since these look pretty. Spoon the mixture carefully into individual dishes and serve immediately or refrigerate up to an hour or so. Serve cold, garnished with reserved berries and mint sprigs if available.

Home-made Meringues

In a large mixer bowl combine the whites of 2 large eggs, a pinch of salt, ½ cup caster sugar and ½ teaspoon of vanilla. Beat together for about 10 minutes or until stiff with peaks that just fold over at the tip when the beater is lifted from them. Shape into about 24 small meringues on a Teflon liner or baking paper. Bake without browning at 100°C for 1–1½ hours, until a meringue, when cooled for 5 minutes, is dry right through. Store cooled meringues in airtight plastic bags or other suitable containers until required (for up to a month).

Rich Mocha Mousse

Serve this deliciously rich mixture in small portions for special occasions!

FOR 8-12 SERVINGS:
500g dark chocolate
½ cup hot water
2 tsp instant coffee
juice & finely grated rind of
   2 medium-sized oranges
3 large eggs, separated

Break chocolate into squares. Heat with the water, instant coffee, orange juice and finely grated orange rind in the microwave, uncovered, on Defrost (30%) power, for 6–7 minutes or until the chocolate has melted. Stir until smooth. Meanwhile, separate the eggs and beat the whites until they form peaks which turn over at the tips when the beater is lifted. Using a whisk, beat the egg yolks into the hot, melted chocolate mixture, then fold in the beaten whites.

Divide mixture between 8–12 small dishes, glasses or coffee cups. Refrigerate for at least 2 hours before serving as is, or with lightly whipped cream, chocolate curls, etc.

NOTE: Refrigerate up to 2 days. With time it will be firmer (but still very good).

Apricot Balls

rind of ½–1 orange
½ cup caster sugar
250g New Zealand* dried apricots,
   chopped
¼ cup orange juice
about 1¾ cups fine desiccated coconut

Remove orange rind with potato peeler, then chop finely with the sugar in a food processor (use more rind for a stronger flavour). Roughly chop the apricots with kitchen scissors, then pulse them with the orange and sugar until finely chopped. Add the juice and process again. Add a cup of the coconut, process, then add more, stopping when mixture may be rolled in balls with wet hands. Shape, roll in coconut, and refrigerate until firm. If not required immediately, freeze in a covered container for up to three months.

*NZ dried apricots are best - sticky and more tender, with a stronger flavour.

Rhubarb, Rhubarb, Rhubarb

Rhubarb Sago

Microwaved sago puddings do not burn on the bottom. Sago makes sour fruit (like rhubarb) less acid, and often more popular with children. Look for sago in Oriental food stores if you cannot find it in your supermarket.

FOR 4 SERVINGS:

¼ cup sago
1½ cups hot tap water
500g (4 cups) chopped rhubarb
½ cup sugar

Put the sago and water in a covered microwave dish about 23cm in diameter. Cover and microwave on High (100%) power for 4 minutes or until the sago mixture has thickened and nearly all the grains of sago have gone clear.

Stir in the rhubarb, chopped into 1cm lengths, and the sugar. Cover again, microwave on High (100%) power for three minutes, then stir well. Cover and cook for 3–4 minutes longer until all rhubarb is hot. Leave to stand for 5 minutes – the rhubarb should finish cooking in this time. Serve warm or cold, alone, with yoghurt, or lightly whipped or runny cream.

Stewed Rhubarb

Chop 500g of rhubarb into 2–4cm lengths and put aside. In a large pot with a close-fitting lid, bring to the boil ½ cup white or brown sugar, ½ cup water, and the finely grated rind of one lemon or orange, or about a teaspoon of freshly grated root ginger, stirring until the sugar dissolves. Lie the rhubarb flat in the syrup, heat quickly until the syrup starts to bubble again, then turn very low, cover with the lid and simmer very gently for 4–6 minutes, until the rhubarb feels tender. Take off the heat, cool the pot in a sink of very cold water and serve warm or cold, with unsweetened yoghurt or runny cream.

Rhubarb Fool

Chop 500g rhubarb in 5mm–1cm pieces, put in a pot with ½ cup white or brown sugar mixed with 2 level teaspoons of cornflour or custard powder, and ¼ cup of water or orange juice. Stir over medium heat until the rhubarb and its sauce thickens, then simmer gently for 5 minutes, stirring often. As soon as the rhubarb breaks up stand the pot in very cold water and mash rhubarb with a potato masher or, for a smoother mixture, purée in a blender or food processor. Whip about ½ cup of cream until it will not pour from the bowl, then fold the whipped cream and cold rhubarb together, spoon into 4 glasses or bowls and refrigerate for at least half an hour before serving.

Creamy Custards

Microwaved custards are smooth and velvety, and may be refrigerated in covered containers for several days.

Vanilla Custard

FOR 4 SERVINGS:
¼ cup custard powder or cornflour
¼ cup sugar
1 egg
2 cups (500ml) milk (any type)
1 tsp vanilla essence
1–2 Tbsp butter

Stir custard powder or cornflour and sugar together in a microwave jug or bowl about 12–14cm across. Break in the egg and add the milk and vanilla. Beat or whisk well, then cook uncovered on High (100%) power for 3 minutes, take out, beat or whisk again, and microwave 1 minute more. Stir in the butter which has been cut into small cubes, and cook for another minute. Repeat, stirring then cooking for a minute, until the custard thickens. Stir well, then lie a plastic bag on the custard, so it covers the whole surface, and no skin can form. Cool the container in cold water, or in the refrigerator or at room temperature, or serve warm.

Caramel Custard

Follow the previous recipe, using brown or dark brown sugar to replace white sugar. Taste while still hot, after it thickens, and stir in 1 or 2 extra tablespoons of (dark) brown sugar if you like.

Chocolate Custard

Add 3 LEVELLED measuring tablespoons of cocoa and ¼ cup of extra sugar to the custard powder or cornflour and sugar mixture and proceed as for vanilla custard.

Banana Custard

Let vanilla or caramel custard cool until you can hold the sides of the container, then slice in one or two bananas, and stir to mix.

Trifle

Put cubes of sponge cake in the bottom of a serving dish (or individual dishes), drizzle with syrup from the fruit to be used, and/or sherry to taste. Top with raspberry jam and drained, cooked sliced peaches, mango, etc. Cover with a layer of vanilla custard and top with whipped cream.

VARIATION: Just before serving, sprinkle with crushed praline (page 50).

Over The Top

Raspberry Sauce

1 cup of fresh or frozen raspberries
2 Tbsp caster sugar
1 tsp cornflour

Purée or mash all ingredients together and bring to the boil so that the sauce thickens slightly. Serve warm or cold, over ice cream etc.

Caramel Sauce

25g butter
½ cup dark or regular brown sugar
¼ cup golden syrup
¼ cup water
pinch of salt
400g can sweetened condensed milk
1 tsp vanilla essence

Melt the butter in a medium-sized pot. Add brown sugar (darker sugar gives more colour and flavour), syrup, water and salt, and bring to the boil, stirring until the sugar has dissolved and the mixture bubbles furiously. Lower heat, add the condensed milk and vanilla, and stir over low heat until well mixed, then take off stove. Serve hot, warm or cold, thinning with hot water, sherry, spirits or liqueurs if sauce is too thick. Use straight away or refrigerate, microwaving to warm when needed.

Chocolate Sauce

2 Tbsp water
¼ cup sugar
100g dark or milk chocolate
¼ cup cream

Heat the water and sugar in a microwave dish on full power for 1½–2 minutes, stirring after a minute, until the sugar has dissolved completely and the syrup has boiled. Break the chocolate into squares or smaller pieces, and tip into the hot syrup. Leave to stand for a minute, then stir until dissolved. Heat for one or more five second bursts only if necessary. Serve warm.

Banana Splits

Kids of all ages love banana splits! For maximum impact, serve them in long sundae dishes, and don't forget the trimmings!

For each banana split, cut a banana lengthwise and place, cut surfaces facing in and ends facing up, on a long sundae dish. Put 2–3 scoops of ice cream between the halved banana, drizzle with chocolate, caramel or raspberry sauce, top with cherries or chopped nuts, and decorate with wafers etc.

Decadent Chocolate Fondue

People of all ages seem to enjoy dipping into a communal pot of chocolate fondue. The dipping fruit disappears like magic, so have plenty!

200–250g dark or milk chocolate
½ cup cream
grated rind of 1 orange or
   1–2 Tbsp brandy, rum or liqueur
   (optional)

Break the chocolate into squares or small pieces, and place in a flat-bottomed microwave dish. Pour the cream over the chocolate. For orange flavouring, finely grate orange rind into the mixture. (A microplane grater does a great job.)

Microwave uncovered on High (100%) power for 2 minutes, leave to stand for 1 minute, then stir until the chocolate and cream are evenly mixed. If any lumps remain, microwave again in 20 second bursts, until lumps disappear when stirred. Stir in spirits, if using.

Pour warm mixture into one or more serving dishes, or rewarm and serve later.

Pile generous amounts of bite-sized pieces of fruit on a flat plate around the hot chocolate dip. (Prepare the fruit ahead and refrigerate in plastic bags, if desired.) Suitable ripe, raw dipping fruits include: apricots, apples, bananas, cherries, grapes, green and yellow kiwifruit, melons, nectarines, oranges, nashi, paw-paw, peaches, pears, plums, pineapple, and strawberries.

NOTE: Two-pronged cocktail forks hold fruit pieces in place better than skewers. Have plenty of paper napkins on hand!

Poached Fruit in Chardonnay Syrup

In cold weather this delicious dried fruit mixture is a reminder of summer! Serve it straight away or refrigerate in a covered jar for several days. Enjoy it warm or cold, alone, or with a slice of plain cake, an after dinner treat, or a selection of cheeses.

FOR ABOUT 4 SERVINGS:

1 cup orange juice
1 cup water
1 cup Chardonnay
½ cup sugar
1–2 cinnamon sticks
3–4 cloves
400g Alison's Choice (dried) Orchard Fruits*
2–3 Tbsp skin-on or blanched almonds
   (optional)

Heat the first six ingredients until the mixture is simmering and the sugar has dissolved, then add all the dried fruit except the dates and simmer for about 10 minutes until the fruit has plumped up nicely. Add dates about 30 seconds before taking off heat. Transfer the fruit, with syrup to cover, to a lidded jar, cool, then refrigerate up to a week or, if using immediately, place in a serving bowl. When required, warm slightly if preferred. Serve fruit with a little syrup.

VARIATION: Replace orange juice with 1 cup of water, the juice of a lemon and a curl of lemon rind if preferred. During storage, fruit should be covered with syrup.

*Look for this fruit mixture in Alison's Choice

Bulk Self-selection bins at New World supermarkets **OR** replace with the same total weight of a mixture of: dried apricots, pears, apple rings, prunes, crystallised pineapple pieces, and crystallised ginger.

Fresh Fruit Ideas

A mixture of three or four fruits looks much more inviting than just one or two. When making a selection consider contrasting colours and textures as well as flavours. Watermelon pieces, large fat blueberries and whole grapes always look great. Large, chunky pieces of fruit look better than small cubes.

Sprinkle cut fruit, especially strawberries, lightly with caster sugar a few minutes before serving, to form juices which glaze the fruit.

Pour chilled Chardonnay (or other interesting) syrup over fresh fruit. Serve cold. Pour sparkling wine over berries in glasses. Garnish with a mint sprig.

Add extra flavour to fruit syrups by adding finely grated orange, lemon rind, fresh root ginger or mint leaves. Try adding a few drops of real vanilla flavour, or try star anise, a cinnamon stick, or freshly grated nutmeg for variety.

Star Attractions

For something so simple to make, these light pastry shapes are an excellent and spectacular way to end a meal.

FOR 4 SERVINGS:
1 sheet pre-rolled frozen flaky pastry
   (about 150g), thawed
2 cups berries, single variety or mixed
   strawberries, raspberries and blueberries
1–2 tablespoons caster sugar
2 tablespoons orange juice
250–300ml cream
1–2 tablespoons caster sugar
finely grated rind of ½ an orange
2–3 drops vanilla essence
icing sugar to dust

Preheat the oven to 200°C. While the oven heats, cut the pastry shapes. Star shapes look extra special (just cut by hand around a cardboard template if you don't have a star cutter big enough), but if you're in a rush then rounds, rectangles (you can get six servings from a sheet with rectangles), or any other shape for that matter, taste just as good. Arrange the pastry on a baking sheet and chill until the oven is ready, then bake for 5–6 minutes until puffed and golden brown. Remove from the oven and cool on a wire rack. (You can do this well in advance if you like.)

Hull and halve or quarter any large strawberries, then place the fruit in a medium-sized bowl. Sprinkle in the sugar (start with the smaller amount and add more if required) and orange juice, then stir gently to combine.

Pour the cream into a large bowl, add sugar to taste, then add the orange rind and vanilla. Beat or whisk until softly whipped (the mixture will just hold its shape but does not look dry).

Assemble just before serving by carefully splitting the pastry shapes into two layers. Place the bottom layer on a flattish plate or bowl and cover with a generous spoonful of the berries. Top the berries with a blob of cream, then carefully place on the pastry cap. Dust with icing sugar (put a little in a fine sieve and tap or shake gently) and serve.

Easy Apple Tartlets

If you use pre-rolled pastry sheets for these, the most complicated step in the preparation of these delicious little tartlets is peeling and slicing a couple of apples!

FOR 4 SERVINGS:
1 sheet pre-rolled flaky pastry
2 Tbsp walnut or pecan pieces
1 Tbsp caster sugar
½ tsp cinnamon
2 medium apples (Granny Smith or Braeburn)
3-4 Tbsp apricot jam, warmed

Sit the pastry on a lightly floured board to thaw and turn the oven on to 190°C (180°C if using fan bake).

Measure the nuts, sugar and cinnamon into a food processor or blender and process until the nuts are finely chopped.

Peel, then halve and core the apples. Lie each half on a board and slice crossways into slices 2–3mm thick. (Depending on the size of the apple you should have 15–20 slices.)

Cut a 2cm wide strip from one side of the pastry sheet so you are left with a rectangle. Cut this into four (equally sized) smaller rectangles and arrange these on a baking sheet. Without cutting right through, run a sharp knife 1cm in from the edge of each rectangle so it marks out a frame. Spread 1–2 tsp of the sugar-nut mixture over each piece of pastry, leaving the border clear, then carefully fan out a sliced apple half on each.

Bake for 15 minutes or until the pastry is golden brown. Leave to stand for 5–10 minutes, then brush each tartlet with a little warmed apricot jam (heat jam for about 30 seconds in the microwave) to glaze, then serve.

Spicy Apple Pie

Using ready-rolled pastry and a food processor, you can make this deliciously spicy pie (with the flavour of Christmas Mincemeat) very quickly.

FOR 6-8 SERVINGS:
2 sheets pre-rolled flaky or puff pastry
½ cup ground almonds (optional)
2 Tbsp plain flour
½ cup raisins or sultanas
¼ cup brown sugar
2 tsp cinnamon
2 tsp mixed spice
¼ tsp ground cloves
1 egg
4 apples (Granny Smith or Braeburn)

Preheat the oven to 200°C with the rack just below the middle. On a floured surface, roll the (fresh or thawed) pastry sheets out more thinly, about 5cm bigger each way. Place one rolled pastry sheet on a baking tray on a non-stick liner or baking paper. Measure all the dry ingredients into a large bowl, mix well with your fingers, and put aside. Beat the egg in a small bowl with a fork.

A food processor does not chop well when overfull, so it is faster and more efficient to mix the filling in two batches. Slice 2 apples, skin and all, into a full-sized food processor fitted with chopping blade. Each apple should be in 10-12 slices. Process in bursts until apple pieces are in small, even chunks but not mushy. Tip into the large bowl with the mixed dry ingredients. Process the remaining apples in the same way. Tip into the bowl, add about a third of the beaten egg, then mix the filling well, using your hand. Pile the filling onto the pastry on the tray, then spread it evenly over the pastry leaving a 2cm strip all round the edge. Brush this strip with some of the remaining egg. Put the second pastry sheet over the apple and pastry, pressing the edges firmly together. Trim the edges evenly without cutting the liner. With a sharp knife, cut a pattern of slashes diagonally across the top crust. Brush the pastry top with the remaining egg.

Bake about 20 minutes at 200°C or until golden brown top and bottom. Dust with icing sugar and serve warm or reheated, with ice cream or lightly whipped cream if desired.

VARIATION: For 2–3 servings, use only one sheet of pastry and make the pie rectangular rather than square. Make half the filling, and use 1 egg, mixing half of it in with the apple. Fold one side of the pastry square over the filling which has been spread on the other half. Seal the open edges and bake as above.

Filo Tartlets with Lemon Cloud Filling

Filo pastry makes quick, crisp, light containers for all sorts of delicious fillings! This one is light and lemony – and made in seconds!

You can make these in small pans for one-bite mouthfuls, or in medium or large muffin or patty pans. Use a piece of thin paper or a tissue to work out what size squares of filo you will need to go across the bottoms and up the sides of your chosen baking pans.

Preheat oven to 180°C. Place a sheet of filo on a dry surface, brush it lightly with unflavoured oil, then cover with another sheet. Using your paper guide, cut two squares for each tart. Take two of the sandwiched squares, place one over the other so the corners form eight-pointed stars, then press them lightly into non-stick sprayed pans. Make as many as required, sandwiching more filo sheets after you have shaped those cut out previously.

Bake for 5-8 minutes, until pastry is evenly golden brown. Lower temperature if corners brown too fast. Take from pans and cool on a rack.

Just before serving, fill tartlets with precooked mixtures and dust with sifted icing sugar. (The icing sugar on moist fillings will disappear.)

LEMON CLOUD FILLING: Make this while the cases cook. Fold together lightly whipped unsweetened cream with good quality lemon honey. Use proportions to suit, starting with half the volume of lemon honey as whipped cream. Top with fresh strawberries if you like. Try passionfruit honey, too.

OTHER FILLINGS: Use the Star Attraction filling (page 24) or cold custard (page 17), or cream cheese beaten with icing sugar and vanilla, brandy or liqueur to taste. Top with sugared or glazed fresh berries or glazed cooked fruit, ready-made cheesecake topping or Christmas mincemeat.

Filo Pear Triangles

These delicious little triangles are flavoured with pears, ginger and nuts.

FOR 4 SERVINGS:
½ slice toast bread
¼ cup roasted cashews
6 pieces crystallised ginger
3 medium-sized firm pears
2 Tbsp sugar
¼ cup sour cream
1 egg yolk
6 sheets filo pastry
oil for brushing

Preheat oven to 180°C. Food process the bread, cashews and ginger until roughly chopped. Add unpeeled pears which have been quartered and cored, then cut in chunks, the sugar, sour cream and egg yolk. Process briefly in bursts, until pear pieces are pea-sized.

Take 3 sheets of the filo pastry and, working quickly on a dry bench, brush the upper side of each one lightly with oil (the whole surface need not be covered). Layer these three sheets, then cut into four even strips crosswise. Put an eighth of the filling at the end of one strip. Fold the end over to form a triangle, then continue folding to encase the filling completely, always forming triangles.

Repeat with remaining pastry and filling.

Brush the folded parcels with a little more oil and bake on an oven tray covered with Teflon or baking paper for about 15 minutes, until golden brown. Serve warm, dusted with icing sugar, with whipped cream or yoghurt.

SPICY APPLE TRIANGLES: Replace pear filling with the apple filling on page 28.

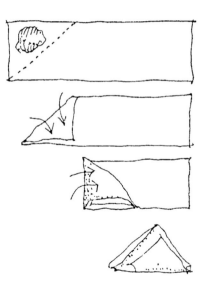

Orange Syrup Cakes

This really easy cake recipe has become a stand by dessert for our entire family! These little cakes are good as is, but if you've got time to soak them with the syrup, it transforms them into a really special dessert.

FOR 6 INDIVIDUAL CAKES:

1 cup sugar
½ cup canola (or other) oil
2 large eggs
finely grated rind of 1 medium orange
½ cup freshly squeezed orange juice
1 tsp vanilla essence
½ tsp salt
1½ cups self-raising flour

ORANGE SYRUP:

¾ cup hot water
¾ cup sugar
finely grated rind of ½ an orange

Preheat the oven to 180°C (or 170°C if using fan bake). Measure sugar, oil, eggs and grated rind into a food processor and blend until pale and creamy. Add orange juice and vanilla and whiz again, then sieve in the salt and flour. Mix just enough to make a fairly smooth batter.

Divide the batter evenly (about ½ cup in each) between six non-stick sprayed plain or fancy muffin tins or other moulds (each should hold 1 cup when full). Bake for 12–15 minutes or until the cakes are golden brown and a skewer poked into the middle of a cake comes out clean.

While the cakes cook prepare the syrup by mixing the hot water, sugar and grated orange rind together in a small microwave bowl or pot. Heat for about 3 minutes on High (100%) power, stirring occasionally, until the mixture boils and the sugar dissolves.

Remove cakes from the oven. Stand for 2–3 minutes before inverting onto a plate or tray and removing the tins. Drizzle the syrup evenly over the bottom and sides of the hot cakes (about 2 Tbsp per little cake).

Leave to stand for at least an hour (overnight is good if possible), before cutting and serving with lightly whipped cream, ice cream or yoghurt.

Quick Chocolate Brownies

Brownies and vanilla ice cream are a delicious traditional combination. Microwaved brownies are soft textured when served the day they are made, and become firmer on standing. They are good both ways – just different!

FOR 6 LARGE OR 12 REGULAR BROWNIES:
½ cup canola or other unflavoured oil
2 large eggs
1 cup sugar
1 tsp vanilla essence
½ tsp salt
½ cup self-raising flour
½ cup plain flour
¼ cup cocoa
¼–½ cup chopped walnuts (optional)

Measure the oil, eggs, sugar, vanilla and salt into a medium-sized bowl and beat well with a fork.

Measure the flours and cocoa into a sieve over the bowl. Sift into the mixture and fold everything together evenly, using a stirrer or rubber scraper. Stir in the nuts if using.

Line a 20cm square (or 21 x 15cm rectangular) microwave container with straight sides at least 6cm high, with a piece of cling film. Tip in the prepared mixture and spread evenly. Cover with a non-stick liner or baking paper. (Covering is important for even rising and cooking.)

Stand the dish on an inverted plate so it is at least 1cm above the cooking surface. Microwave on High (100%) power for 4–7 minutes, checking every minute after 4 minutes. Do not worry if the surface looks rather uneven, but don't take the brownies out of the microwave until they are dry on top. Cool in cooking container, then turn out onto a cutting board. When cold, cut into bars or other shapes.

Dust the top with icing sugar, or turn the cut pieces in sifted icing sugar so all surfaces are covered. Serve with vanilla ice cream.

NOTE: If the top is not covered during cooking, brownies will take longer to cook and the top may not cook (and rise) evenly. We use a lidded rectangular plastic storage container (without its lid) to cook our brownies, and find it very successful.

VARIATION: If preferred, bake brownies in a 20cm square baking-paper lined pan at 180°C for 20–30 minutes or until a toothpick comes out clean.

Fruity Steamed Pudding

This pudding has a lovely flavour and wonderful aroma. It contains no flour, butter or oil, and is quick to mix. Reheat leftovers or eat cold, as with fruit cake.

FOR 4-6 SERVINGS:

1¼ cups instant rolled oats
1 cup milk
2 household dessertspoons golden syrup
500g (4 cups) good quality mixed fruit
1 tsp cinnamon
1 tsp mixed spice
½ tsp ground cloves
½ tsp lemon essence
½ tsp salt
1 large egg
1 tsp baking soda

First of all, measure the oats into a fairly large mixing bowl, pour the milk over them, and leave to stand for a few minutes while you get out everything else. Put the dried fruit in a sieve and run boiling or very hot water over it. Drain well and tip it on top of the oats, without stirring. Drizzle the measured golden syrup over the hot fruit so it softens. Add the flavourings, salt and egg, then mix everything together thoroughly with a fork. Measure the baking soda, tip it into your palm, press with the back of a spoon to make sure there are no lumps, then sprinkle it over the mixture and stir in well.

Lightly but evenly spray a six-cup microwave ring pan with non-stick spray. Pour the wet-looking pudding mixture into this and cover the top lightly with a paper towel or a piece of greaseproof or baking paper. Place it on an upturned dinner plate (so the base of the pudding cooks faster) and microwave at Medium-High (70%) power for 15 minutes. Leave to stand for 5 minutes before turning out onto a flat plate. (This is a little faster than making individual puddings.)

OR spray 6-8 teacups or cup-sized ramekins lightly but evenly with non-stick spray. Divide mixture between these, so each is about ¾ full. Level the tops, and cover loosely with squares of baking paper. Place in a circle on the turntable, about 5cm from the outer edge, and microwave for 12–14 minutes on Medium-High (70%) power, until the tops of the puddings have set and seem cooked, although they will still feel soft. Leave to stand for 5 minutes before turning out. Pudding colour darkens on standing. If they don't come out easily when upturned, slip a thin bladed knife down the side of each so they slide out.

Serve with lightly whipped cream, or bought or homemade custard (page 17).

Bourbon Street Bread Pudding

Forget your previous thoughts about bread puddings! This one, with its wonderful sauce, is rich, sinfully delicious, and addictive!

FOR 4 SERVINGS:
25g butter
¾ cup milk
¼ cup cream
½ cup sugar
1 large egg
white of 1 large egg
1 tsp vanilla essence
½ tsp cinnamon or mixed spice
½ tsp grated nutmeg
75g very dry bread (2 bread rolls)
¼ cup sultanas or currants

SAUCE:
50g butter
¾ cup icing sugar
yolk of 1 large egg
2–3 Tbsp rum, whisky or bourbon

In a large bowl melt the butter on High (100%) power for about a minute. Stir in all remaining ingredients except the bread and dried fruit, and mix well, using a fork. Add the bread, crumbled or cut in 1cm cubes, and the dried fruit. Leave to stand for a few minutes while the bread softens, then mix again. The mixture should be firm enough to keep a rounded shape in four microwave-proof bowls, ramekins or cups. Spoon in mixture so each container is no more than three-quarters full. Microwave uncovered at Medium (50%) power for 8–10 minutes or until firm. Serve warm, with the warm sauce drizzled over the top.

SAUCE: In a medium-sized bowl melt the butter on High (100%) power for 1 minute. Beat in icing sugar and egg yolk. Microwave for 30 seconds or until the liquid bubbles around the edges. Cool, then stir in the whisky, rum or bourbon.

Shortcut Apple Crumble

Unbelievably quick and easy, this crumble has only two ingredients. Proportions need not be exact. They are listed just to give you an idea of quantities.

FOR 2 SERVINGS:
(USE DOUBLE QUANTITIES FOR 4 PEOPLE)
1–2 cups hot, cooked, unsweetened apple or a 400g can of diced apple
¾–1 cup muesli*

* Use Alison's Apricot and Almond Muesli, Alison's Cranberry Crunch, or Alison's Decadent Delight (in a foil pack), available from New World stores. (Only muesli with a crumbled biscuity texture works for this pudding.)

Preheat the oven to 170–180°C. Heat contents of a 400g can of diced apple in a microwave dish in a microwave or in a pot. Add a little orange juice if it seems dry, and heat until warmed through.

Put the hot, cooked apple (and juice) in a well-sprayed baking dish (as for a traditional apple crumble). Sprinkle evenly with muesli, pushing down visible dried fruit into the apple, so it does not burn. Cover loosely with a piece of foil or a Teflon liner and bake for 10 minutes, then uncover and bake for 5–10 minutes longer. Watch that the topping browns only to the golden brown stage, but not too much.

Serve warm with ice cream, sour or fresh cream, plain yoghurt or custard (page 17).

NOTE: For home-cooked apple, coarsely grate (or chop in a food processor) unpeeled Granny Smiths or other apples. Heat in a covered microwave-proof dish (in which the pudding can later be baked), or simmer in a covered pot with ½ cup of orange juice until tender and juicy. (3 cups of raw grated apple yields about 2 cups of cooked apple.)

Instant Coffee Gateau

This makes an excellent dessert for entertaining, since it can be prepared the night before you need it. Leftovers may be enjoyed for a couple of days after this, too.

Avoid the temptation to serve this cake only a few hours after you have made it, or you will be disappointed. It needs at least 12 hours to absorb moisture from the cream and syrup.

FOR 8 SERVINGS:

1 unfilled sponge sandwich 20-23cm
   across or
   one layer of slab sponge, 30 x 25cm
1 Tbsp instant coffee
¾ cup sugar
¼ cup water
½ tsp rum or brandy essence or
   2 Tbsp rum or brandy
1½ cups cream, whipped
4–6 Zespri Green or Gold kiwifruit
about ½ cup chopped walnuts or
   slivered toasted almonds

Split each layer of sponge, making two thinner layers. Use three layers for this cake. (Layers may be patched, and unused sponge frozen for later use.) Use slab cake to make a long, rectangular log to cut in slices.

Boil instant coffee, sugar and water together, stirring constantly until sugar has dissolved completely, then simmer for 2 minutes, cool and add essence or spirits. Whip the cream until it is just thick enough not to pour from the bowl.

Place a layer of sponge on a serving dish, drizzle or brush a quarter of the syrup over it, then top with half the thinly peeled, sliced kiwifruit and no more than a quarter of the whipped cream. Drizzle or brush the same quantity of syrup over the next layer of cake while it is lying on the working surface, then place it, coffee side down, over the cream.

Repeat, using the remaining syrup and fruit, and the third layer of cake, then spread the sides and top of the cake with as much of the remaining cream as necessary. Sprinkle nuts over sides (and top if desired) of the cake. Cover carefully and refrigerate for at least 12 hours (preferably 24) before serving. Cut in wedges or slices to serve, with extra fruit to garnish if you like.

VARIATION: Decorate the top of the gateau with overlapping slices of fruit just before serving **OR** replace kiwifruit with sliced strawberries **OR** prepare gateau as above but without putting fruit in the filling. Pile grapes or berries on top if desired.

Black Forest Roll

This easy and reliable sponge roll has been a stand by in our house for decades, celebrating many birthdays and special occasions. We can take the cake from the oven less than twenty minutes after we start mixing.

3 large eggs
½ cup sugar
¼ tsp salt
½ cup flour
2 Tbsp cocoa
1 tsp baking powder
1 Tbsp boiling water

Filling, see following

Heat oven to 230°C (or 220°C fanbake), with the rack just below the centre of oven. With an electric beater, beat eggs, sugar and salt together in a fairly large bowl, until mixture is thick, creamy and pale. (Use room temperature eggs and don't hurry the beating.) Meanwhile, line the bottom and sides of a fairly large (about 22 x 30cm) sponge roll tin with a piece of baking paper cut at the corners where the edges fold up.

Measure the flour, cocoa and baking powder into a sieve over a piece of paper, then lift paper, return mixture to the sieve, and sift it on to the thick egg mixture. Fold in carefully but thoroughly until no pockets of dry ingredients remain. Add the boiling water and fold it in too, then spread the thick mixture evenly in the lined tin.

Bake for 7–10 minutes or until the centre springs back when pressed lightly. (Take care not to cook longer than necessary or the sponge will shrink.)

While sponge roll cooks, lightly butter another piece of baking paper or a large Teflon liner. Sprinkle caster sugar evenly over this, shaking off excess. Quickly turn the cooked cake out onto this surface, bottom up. Lift off the baking paper and cool the sponge on the sugared surface on a cooling rack.

FILLING AND DECORATING: When cooled to room temperature, spread with raspberry jam, then whipped rum cream. (Beat 1 cup of cream with ¼ cup icing sugar and 1–2 Tbsp rum until thick.) Over this sprinkle well-drained canned or bottled cherries or about a cup of fresh or thawed raspberries.

Roll up, starting from a short end, lifting the paper or liner to help you. Keep the paper/liner rolled around the roll until you are ready to serve it, then serve, join-side down, as is, or dusted with icing sugar. Add chocolate or white chocolate curls for extra decoration, if you like.

VARIATION: If preferred, cut cream-topped sponge in two or three pieces and layer these, instead of forming a roll.

Uncooked Coconut Ice

This is easy enough for children to make, but popular with adults too.

2 cups desiccated coconut
2 cups icing sugar
½ a 400g can sweetened condensed milk
1 tsp vanilla essence
¼ tsp raspberry essence (optional)
4–5 drops of red food colouring
extra coconut for coating

Measure coconut and icing sugar into a bowl. Tip in condensed milk and vanilla, then mix well.

Sprinkle some of the extra coconut on a flat sheet of plastic. Press out half the mixture (about 20cm square) on the coconut. Add the raspberry essence and enough food colouring to give a pale pink colour to the mixture left in the bowl, mix in, then shape as previously.

Lay the pink layer on top of the white layer. Sprinkle a little extra coconut on top. Refrigerate for 15 minutes or longer, then cut into squares with a wet knife. Refrigerate until required, and eat after a few hours.

Failsafe Fudge

250g dark, milk or white chocolate
½ a 400g can sweetened condensed milk
½ tsp vanilla essence
¼–½ cup chopped glacé cherries or dried fruit (optional)
¼–½ cup lightly roasted, chopped almond, walnuts, pecans etc. (optional)

Break the chocolate in squares and put it in a medium-sized microwave dish. Add the condensed milk and stir, then heat on Medium (50%) power for one minute bursts, stirring between each. Stop as soon as chocolate is completely melted (3-4 minutes in total).

Stir in the vanilla essence and the extras (if any) of your choice, then pour the fudge into a baking paper, Teflon or cling film lined tin and smooth the top if required. We usually use something about 20 x 20cm but for thicker fudge use something smaller.

Cool until firm in the fridge or freezer (this should take about 20-40 minutes, depending on the temperature, thickness etc.), then cut into serving-sized squares and enjoy. Store leftovers in a closed container in the fridge.

Fabulous Fudge

This microwaved fudge is easier and more reliable than traditionally cooked fudge.

100g butter
1 cup sugar
¼ cup golden syrup
400g can sweetened condensed milk
1 tsp vanilla essence

Mix all ingredients except vanilla in a large bowl resistant to high heat. Microwave on High (100%) power, stirring every 2 minutes until sugar has dissolved, the mixture has bubbled vigorously all over its surface, and a little dropped in cold water forms a soft ball (this is when the mixture which has been dropped in a glass flattens, but stays in a roundish ball after you have shaped it). This usually takes about 10–12 minutes.

Add vanilla and beat for about 5 minutes, until mixture suddenly starts to keep its shape and loses its gloss. Before it sets, quickly turn onto a lightly buttered flat surface or 20cm square pan. When cool and firm, cut into squares.

VARIATION: For Chocolate Fudge, add ¼ cup cocoa powder to the sugar. For Nut Fudge, stir in ¼ cup chopped walnuts after you start beating.

Praline Shards

1 cup sugar
½ cup nuts, such as slivered almonds,
  chopped macadamias, chopped
  hazelnuts, peanuts

Heat the sugar in a clean, dry non-stick frypan over a medium heat without stirring at all. As the pan heats and the sugar begins to melt, shake and tilt the pan so it melts evenly. After a few minutes the melted sugar will begin to brown. As soon as the sugar has all melted and is an even light golden-brown colour, add the nuts.

Shake and tilt the pan to combine nuts with the caramel. Taking great care not to burn yourself, carefully pour hot caramel mixture onto a non-stick liner, or baking paper, on an oven tray. Carefully spread out any large clusters of nuts. The mixture should slowly spread out until it is about 5mm thick.

When cool, break the praline into long shards. Serve with coffee or as a garnish for other desserts. Store in clean, dry, airtight containers and use within a week.

NOTE: Do not overcook, as dark caramel develops a bitter taste.

Cherry Truffles

These not-too-rich little balls have been favourites in our house for thirty years!

200g wine biscuits, crushed
1½ cups desiccated coconut
12–20 glacé cherries
100g melted butter
½ of a 400g can sweetened condensed milk
1 tsp almond essence (optional)
¼ cup sherry, brandy or Kirsch
extra coconut for coating

Crush broken biscuits finely in a food processor or use a rolling pin to crush biscuits in a plastic bag. Mix the crumbs, coconut and chopped cherries.

Heat the butter in a small pan or microwave bowl until liquid. Take off heat and stir in the condensed milk. Add almond essence if you are not using the Kirsch. Mix in the sherry, brandy or Kirsch, then pour mixture into crumbs and coconut and combine, by hand or in the food processor.

Roll into small balls and coat with extra coconut. Refrigerate or freeze.

Chocolate Coconut Balls

This is our tried and true family favourite chocolate ball recipe.

½ of a 250g packet wine biscuits
100g butter
¼ cup cocoa
1 cup icing sugar
½ cup desiccated coconut
2 Tbsp sherry or orange juice
extra coconut for rolling

Put the biscuits in a plastic bag and bang with a rolling pin until completely crushed, or chop the broken biscuits in a food processor.

Soften the butter, taking care not to melt it. Mix with all remaining ingredients (except the extra coconut) in a bowl or food processor. Mix well, then cool the mixture for about 10 minutes in the refrigerator before rolling into small balls.

Roll balls in extra coconut and store in the refrigerator or freezer.

Chocolate Liqueur Truffles

Ultra rich and smooth, these decadent truffles are wonderful after a special occasion dinner.

150g dark chocolate
2 Tbsp rum, brandy or orange liqueur
2 Tbsp butter
1 egg yolk
¼ cup cocoa

Break chocolate into squares and put in a round microwave-proof or heat-proof glass container with the spirit or liqueur of your choice. Microwave uncovered on Defrost (30%) power for 3–4 minutes, or in a bowl over boiling water until the chocolate has melted enough to be mixed smoothly with the liqueur.

Stir in the butter and egg yolk until well combined. (The melted chocolate will melt the butter.) Refrigerate until firm enough to shape into walnut-sized balls, then drop a few at a time into the cocoa in a bowl, and rotate gently until coated. Lift out with a spoon and put on a flat plate or in small cases.

Refrigerate or freeze in a covered container until required. Serve chilled.

Chocolate Dipped Delights

Chocolate dipped foods always look enticing and are quick and easy to do! Try coating (or partly coating) dried apricots, Brazil and other nuts, grapes and strawberries.

Warm broken squares of dark, milk, or white chocolate in a small microwave bowl, in 30 second bursts, at Medium (50%) power, stopping as soon as the chocolate is smooth and semi-liquid when stirred. If necessary, thin the melted chocolate with Kremelta (Copha). Only use a very small amount, as too much will make the chocolate runny and slow down setting. (Add a piece the size of a green pea, then more if needed.) For fast setting, dip dry, chilled foods.

After dipping, hold the food above the container of melted chocolate to catch drips, then cool on a Teflon non-stick liner or a piece of plastic. Refrigerate or stand in a cool place until set. Chocolate dipped strawberries and grapes should be eaten within a few hours but nuts and dried fruits may be refrigerated in a covered container for some weeks.

Spiced Prunes In Port

Prunes soaked in port are wonderful! They will keep in an unsealed jar in the refrigerator for months, if they get the chance – ready for serving after dinner with cheese, spooned over vanilla ice cream, or snacked on by a deserving cook! The liquid becomes more syrupy with longer storage.

Loosely fill the jar you want to use with good quality prunes. Take them out again, put them in a pot or bowl and cover with boiling water. Leave for 5 minutes – no longer – then pour off and discard the water.

Put the drained prunes back in the jar, adding one or more of the following if you like complex flavours: a piece of cinnamon stick, a few cloves, some juniper berries, crushed cardamom berries, a couple of petals of star anise, and/or a few strips of orange or lemon rind. Leave some space at the top of the jar.

Pour port over the prunes so they are well covered, since they will soak up some port on standing. Cover with a well-fitting lid, and leave at room temperature for 12–36 hours before refrigerating or using.

Say Cheese...

A cheese board is a great alternative (or even an additional finishing touch) to a 'traditional' sweet dessert, and, from a cook's point of view, couldn't be much easier.

Although we are now spoilt for choice, simplicity is often the order of the day for a successful cheese board. Three or perhaps four different cheeses, say a blue (and you can choose from mild or strong to suit your taste), a hardish cheese (like a cheddar, Edam, Gouda, Gruyere etc., or even something smoked) and a soft 'fresh' cheese (a

Camembert or Brie) are all that are required. Like red wine, most cheese is better served at room temperature, so it's a good idea to remove it from the fridge (take them out of tight wrappers so they can 'breathe' too) before you sit down to your main course.

Absolute purists assert that the cheese is enough on its own, but some very plain crackers or bread and perhaps a few grapes, some dried fruit and/or a few nuts make good accompaniments too.

Published by Hyndman Publishing,
325 Purchas Road,
RD2 Amberley, 7482

ISBN: 1-877168-70-X
TEXT: ©Simon & Alison Holst
DESIGNER: Rob Di Leva
PHOTOGRAPHER: Lindsay Keats, except page 12
– Sal Criscillo
HOME ECONOMISTS: Simon & Alison Holst, Hilary Wilson-Hill
PROPS: Fiona Stewart
PRINTING: Spectrum Print

The recipes in this book have been carefully tested by the authors. The publisher and the authors have made every effort to ensure that the instructions are accurate and safe, but they cannot accept liability for any resulting injury or loss or damage to property, whether direct or consequential.

Because ovens and microwave ovens vary so much, you should take the cooking times suggested in recipes as guides only. The first time you make a recipe, check it at intervals to make sure it is not cooking faster, or more slowly than expected.

Always follow the detailed instructions given by manufacturers of your appliances and equipment, rather than the more general instructions given in these recipes.

Important Information:

For best results, use a standard metric (250ml) measuring cup and metric measuring spoons when you use these recipes:
1 tablespoon holds 15ml and
1 teaspoon holds 5ml.

All the cup and spoon measures in the recipes are level, unless otherwise stated. Sets of measuring cups make it easier to measure ¼ and ½ cup quantities.

Larger amounts of butter are given by weight. Use pack markings as a guide. Small amounts of butter are measured using spoons (1 tablespoon of butter weighs about 15 grams).

Abbreviations used:

ml	millilitre
tsp	teaspoon
Tbsp	tablespoon
g	gram
°C	Celsius
cm	centimetre

INDEX

Knives by Mail Order

For about 20 years Alison has imported her favourite, very sharp kitchen knives from Switzerland. They keep their edges well, are easy to sharpen, a pleasure to use, and make excellent gifts.

VEGETABLE KNIFE $8.00
Ideal for cutting and peeling vegetables, these knives have a straight edged 85mm blade and black (dishwasher-proof) nylon handle. Each knife comes in an individual plastic sheath.

BONING/UTILITY KNIFE $9.50
Excellent for boning chicken and other meats, and/or for general kitchen duties. Featuring a 103mm blade that curves to a point and a dishwasher-proof, black nylon handle, each knife comes in a plastic sheath.

SERRATED KNIFE $9.50
These knives are unbelievably useful. They are perfect for cutting cooked meats, ripe fruit and vegetables, and slicing bread and baking. Treated carefully, these blades stay sharp for years. The serrated 110mm blade is rounded at the end with a black (dishwasher-proof) nylon handle and each knife comes in an individual plastic sheath.

THREE-PIECE SET $22.00
This three-piece set includes a vegetable knife, a serrated knife (as described above) and a right-handed potato peeler with a matching black handle, presented in a white plastic wallet.

GIFT BOXED KNIFE SET $44.00
This set contains five knives plus a matching right-handed potato peeler. There is a straight bladed vegetable knife and a serrated knife (as above), as well as a handy 85mm serrated blade vegetable knife, a small (85mm) utility knife with a pointed tip and a smaller (85mm) serrated knife. These elegantly presented sets make ideal gifts.

SERRATED CARVING KNIFE $28.50
This fabulous knife cuts beautifully and is a pleasure to use, it's ideal for carving or cutting fresh bread. The 21cm serrated blade does not require sharpening. Once again the knife has a black moulded, dishwasher safe handle and comes in a plastic sheath.

COOK'S KNIFE $35.00
An excellent all-purpose kitchen knife. With a well balanced 19cm wedge-shaped blade and a contoured black nylon handle, these knives make short work of slicing and chopping, and have come out on top of their class in several comparative tests. Each dishwasher-safe knife comes with its own plastic sheath.

STEEL $20.00
These steels have a 20cm 'blade' and measure 33cm in total. With its matching black handle the steel is an ideal companion for your own knives, or as a gift. Alison gets excellent results using these steels. N.B. Not for use with serrated knives.

PROBUS SPREADER/SCRAPER $7.50
After her knives, these are the most used tools in Alison's kitchen! With a comfortable plastic handle, metal shank and flexible plastic blade (suitable for use on non-stick surfaces), these are excellent for mixing muffin batters, stirring and scraping bowls, spreading icings, turning pikelets etc., etc....

NON-STICK TEFLON LINERS
Re-usable SureBrand Teflon liners are another essential kitchen item – they really help avoid the frustration of stuck-on baking, roasting or frying. Once you've used them, you'll wonder how you did without!

Round tin liner	
(for 15–23cm tins)	$6.50
(for 23–30cm tins)	$9.50
Square tin liner	
(for 15–23cm tins)	$6.50
(for 23–30cm tins)	$9.50
Ring tin liner	
(for 23cm tins)	$6.95
Baking sheet liner	
(33 × 44cm)	$13.95

All prices include GST. Prices current at time of publishing, subject to change without notice. Please add $5.00 post & packing to all orders (any number of items).

Make cheques payable to Alison Holst Mail Orders and post to:
Alison Holst Mail Orders
FREEPOST 124807
PO Box 17016
Wellington
Or visit us at www.holst.co.nz